The Unofficial
Harry Potter
Beauty Potions Book

Published in 2015 by
razzberry books
email: info@razzberrybooks.com

Printed in the United States of America

ISBN-13: 978-0692440322
ISBN-10: 0692440321

Table of Contents

Every witch and wizard, grab your mixing bowls, because in these pages, you're going to learn how to whip up the most magical beauty concoctions allowed in the Muggle world. From Slytherin to Smoother Skin Sugar Scrub to Butterbeer Body Butter, there's something for everyone (even Squibs).

Whirl up some mystical gifts or keep these magic potions all for yourself. Either way, you'll feel like you just won the Quidditch finals, or aced your OWLs.

Get out your cauldrons and let's begin!

Amortentia Lotion

Yearning after some one? Then look no further than this love potion in a lotion. Scented with ylang ylang and rose, hold their heart with the most seductive fragrance in Amortentia.

Ingredients:
1/2 cup Olive Oil
1/4 cup Coconut Oil
1/4 cup Beeswax
1 teaspoon Vitamin E Oil
6 drops of Ylang Ylang Essential Oil
5 drops of Rose Absolute Essential Oil
The tiniest pinch of Red Beet Powder for a natural pink color

Directions:
Combine all ingredients inside a quart-sized mason jar. Leave the lid loosely placed on the jar. Place the mason jar inside a pan with 1 inch of water in it.

Turn the heat on medium and stir the ingredients until completely melted.

Pour the finished product in smaller mason jars or bottles.

Felix Felicis Lotion

Ever wanted to know what euphoria feels like? Want to have everything in your life go exactly right? Then try Felix Felicis lotion, scented with grapefruit and bergamot, and your spirits are guaranteed to soar.

Ingredients:
1/2 cup Olive Oil
1/4 cup Coconut Oil
1/4 cup Beeswax
1 teaspoon Vitamin E Oil
5 drops of Grapefruit Essential Oil
5 drops of Bergamot Essential Oil
2-3 drops of yellow food coloring

Directions:
Combine all ingredients inside a quart-sized mason jar. Leave the lid loosely placed on the jar. Place the mason jar inside a pan with 1 inch of water in it.

Turn the heat on medium and stir the ingredients until completely melted.

Pour the finished product in smaller mason jars or bottles.

Time Turner Lotion

Noticed time slipping through your fingers?
Want to just spin the dial and go back?
Try Time Turner Anti-Aging Lotion to start seeing
that change. Geranium and Lavender essential oils
are used to add back that elasticity
and youthful glow to your skin.

Ingredients:
1/2 cup Olive Oil
1/4 cup Coconut Oil
1/4 cup Beeswax
1 teaspoon Vitamin E Oil
6 drops of Lavender Essential Oil
6 drops of Geranium Essential Oil

Directions:
Combine all ingredients inside a quart-sized mason jar. Leave the lid loosely placed on the jar. Place the mason jar inside a pan with 1 inch of water in it.

Turn the heat on medium and stir the ingredients until completely melted.

Pour the finished product in smaller mason jars or bottles.

Erised Lotion

Ever looked in a mirror and saw everything you ever wanted right before your eyes? It's not unattainable anymore. Erised is scented with jasmine and orange to make any of your days feel romantic and beautiful.

Ingredients:
1/2 cup Olive Oil
1/4 cup Coconut Oil
1/4 cup Beeswax
1 teaspoon Vitamin E Oil
3 drops of Jasmine Essential Oil
2 drops of Mandarin Orange Essential Oil
Purple Food Coloring (1 drop of blue and 2 drops of red)

Directions:
Combine all ingredients inside a quart-sized mason jar. Leave the lid loosely placed on the jar. Place the mason jar inside a pan with 1 inch of water in it.

Turn the heat on medium and stir the ingredients until completely melted.

Pour the finished product in smaller mason jars or bottles.

Espresso Patronum Sugar Scrub

Loaded with antioxidants to prevent aging, and full of great exfoliants, the Espresso Patronum Sugar Scrub is every coffee lover's dream!

Waking you up with a zing, you'll feel like you've just had a shot of Felix Felicis.

Ingredients:
1 cup Cane Sugar
1/4 cup Olive Oil
2 tablespoon Raw Honey
2 teaspoon Dried Rosemary
15 drops of coffee extract
15 drops of vanilla

Directions:
Mix all ingredients (except essential oils) together.

Add essential oils and stir until combined.

Aloha-homora Sugar Scrub

Open a door to the islands with the Aloha-homora Sugar Scrub. Blended with coconut oil and cocoa butter, your skin will feel moisturized and carefree.

Ingredients:
1 cup Cane Sugar
1/4 cup Olive Oil
2 tablespoon Raw Honey
2 teaspoon Dried Rosemary
15 drops of coconut oil
15 drops of cocoa butter

Directions:
Mix all ingredients (except essential oils) together.

Add essential oils and stir until combined.

Gringott's Good as Gold
Sugar Scrub Cubes

Bank account got you down? Not enough Galleons in your purse? No matter, scented with ginger and orange, and a great exfoliant, Gringott's Good as Gold Sugar Scrub Cubes will keep your spirits strong and uplifted and that is worth every Knut.

Ingredients:
1/4 cup Coconut Oil
1 cup Brown Sugar
1/2 cup Unscented Soap, Shredded
Ginger oil
Orange oil

Directions:
Put the shredded soap and coconut oil in a microwavable bowl. Microwave in 20 second intervals, stirring between each interval. Keep doing this until the soap is completely melted.

Stir in ginger and orange oils.

Pour into molds.

When the scrubs are firm, pop them out of the molds and store in a lidded container.
When you're ready to shower, take a couple with you and run under the water for a few seconds and crush them up. Scrub away!

Deluminator Sugar Scrub Cubes

Do you sometimes want to just turn out all the lights
and let all your cares drift away? With the
Deluminator Sugar Scrub Cubes, you can do just that.
Get deliciously smooth skin and a relaxed mindset
with just one product.

Ingredients:
1/4 cup Coconut Oil
1 cup Brown Sugar
1/2 cup Unscented Soap, Shredded
Roman Chamomile oil

Directions:
Put the shredded soap and coconut oil in a microwavable bowl. Microwave in 20 second intervals, stirring between each interval. Keep doing this until the soap is completely melted.

Stir in roman chamomile oil.

Pour into molds.

When the scrubs are firm, pop them out of the molds and store in a lidded container.
When you're ready to shower, take a couple with you and run under the water for a few seconds and crush them up. Scrub away!

Fawkes' Phoenix Tears
Sugar Scrub Cubes

Do you have a lightning bolt scar that just won't go away? Then look no further than Fawkes' Phoenix Tears Sugar Scrub Cubes, blended with clary sage and lavender, you will soon be on your way to softer skin.

Ingredients:
1/4 cup Coconut Oil
1 cup Brown Sugar
1/2 cup Unscented Soap, Shredded
Clary Sage Oil
Lavender Oil

Directions:
Put the shredded soap and coconut oil in a microwavable bowl. Microwave in 20 second intervals, stirring between each interval. Keep doing this until the soap is completely melted.

Stir in clary sage and lavender oils.

Pour into molds.

When the scrubs are firm, pop them out of the molds and store in a lidded container.

When you're ready to shower, take a couple with you and run under the water for a few seconds and crush them up. Scrub away!

Dirigible Plums Bubble Bath

Want to float away on a cloud and feel like you can accept the extraordinary?

The Dirigible Plum Bubble Bath, scented with plum oil and jasmine, will guide your thoughts to relaxation.

Ingredients:
1/2 cup Light Almond Oil
1/4 cup Honey
1/2 cup Mild Liquid Hand Soap
1 Egg White
Jasmine Essential Oil
Plum Fragrance Oil

Directions:
Combine and pour 1/2 cup under running bath water. Keep remaining mixture in the refrigerator.

Golden Egg Bubble Bath

Missing the song of the merpeople? Take your Golden Egg Bubble Bath, listen hard, and breathe in the rich fragrances of lavender and sweet orange oils. You'll quickly float down to the Black Lake.

Ingredients:
1/2 cup Light Almond Oil
1/4 cup Honey
1/2 cup Mild Liquid Hand Soap
1 Egg White
Lavender Oil
Sweet Orange Oil

Directions:
Combine and pour 1/2 cup under running bath water. Keep remaining mixture in the refrigerator.

Goblet of Fire Bubble Bath

The Triwizard Tournament is here and what better way to get your name chosen than to have Goblet of Fire Bubble Bath. Blended with Rosewood and Neroli, each bath will make you feel like a champion.

Ingredients:
1/2 cup Light Almond Oil
1/4 cup Honey
1/2 cup Mild Liquid Hand Soap
1 Egg White
Essential oils

Directions:
Combine and pour 1/2 cup under running bath water. Keep remaining mixture in the refrigerator.

Licorice Wand Lip Scrub

Give your tired lips a treat with Licorice Wand Lip Scrub. Blended with anise, the natural sugars will give your lips a nice glossy finish.

This scrub exfoliates away dead skin, leaving lips super soft and luscious.

Ingredients:
3 tablespoon Castor Sugar
3 tablespoon Jojoba Oil
A few drops of Aniseed Oil

Directions:
Pour oils into a small bowl. Mix in the sugar.

Pour into a small container. Old lip gloss containers work great for this.

Dementor's Kiss Lip Scrub

A fate worse than death awaits your dry skin with Dementor's Kiss Lip Scrub. Peppermint oil and sugar will wash it all away leaving lips kissably smooth.

This scrub exfoliates away dead skin, leaving lips super soft and luscious.

Ingredients:
3 tablespoon Castor Sugar
3 tablespoon Jojoba Oil
2-3 drops Peppermint Oil
A pinch of Red Beet Powder for a natural red color

Directions:
Pour oil into a small bowl. Mix in the sugar. Add peppermint oil and coloring.

Pour into a small container. Old lip gloss containers work great for this.

Fiendfyre Lip Scrub

Give your lips a magical makeover with Fiendfyre Lip Scrub. Peach flavored with natural sugars, your lips will look and taste bewitching.

This scrub exfoliates away dead skin, leaving lips super soft and luscious.

Ingredients:
3 tablespoon Castor Sugar
3 tablespoon Jojoba Oil
2-3 drops of Peach Flavoring Oil

Directions:
Pour oil into a small bowl. Mix in the sugar. Add peach oil.

Pour into a small container. Old lip gloss containers work great for this.

Pensieve Shower Jelly

Need to siphon some excess thoughts away? Want to
collect memories and put them in a jar? Get the next
best thing with Pensieve Shower Jelly
and feel your mind clear.

Ingredients:
2 boxes of Unflavored Gelatin or Agar-Agar
1 cup Clear Shower Gel or Body Wash
2-3 drops of Blue Food Coloring
2-3 drops of Eucalyptus Essential Oil
2-3 drops of Peppermint Essential Oil

Directions:
Boil water according to the directions on your box of gelatin/agar-agar.

When the water has reached a rolling boil, slowly whisk in the gelatin/agar-agar. Then pour in the shower gel/body wash.

Stir in the food coloring and oils.

Pour the mixture into a bowl and refrigerate for at least 6 hours.

Remove the mixture from the fridge and scoop into glass jars.

Remembrall Shower Jelly

Feel like you are forgetting something? Use
Rememberall Shower Jelly scented with marjoram
and rosemary and get back all your lost thoughts.

Ingredients:
2 boxes of Unflavored Gelatin or Agar-Agar (for a vegan version)
1 cup Clear Shower Gel or Body Wash
2-3 drops of Red Food Coloring
2-3 drops of Marjoram Essential Oil
2-3 drops of Rosemary Essential Oil

Directions:
Boil water according to the directions on your box of gelatin/agar-agar.

When the water has reached a rolling boil, slowly whisk in the gelatin/agar-agar. Then pour in the shower gel/body wash.

Stir in the food coloring and oils.

Pour the mixture into a bowl and refrigerate for at least 6 hours.

Remove the mixture from the fridge and scoop into glass jars.

Trelawney's Tea Tree Body Wash

You want to study the most difficult magical art of divination? Your tea leaves preventing you from being receptive of your future? Then look no further than Trelawney's Tea Tree Body Wash scented with tea tree oil and clove. You will find all your mysteries come to light.

Ingredients:
2/3 cup Liquid Castile Soap
1/4 cup Raw, Unfiltered Honey
2 teaspoons Oil (jojoba, almond, sesame, or olive)
1 teaspoon Vitamin E Oil
25 drops of Tea Tree Oil
25 drops of Clove oil

Directions:
Pour all ingredients into a bottle and shake vigorously. To use, squirt directly onto a loofa, washcloth, or directly onto skin.

Slug Club Body Wash

Want to fit in with the people who will be outstanding? To be a part of Hogwarts' brightest and best? Scented with bergamot and coriander, the Official Slug Club Body Wash is your first step into the spotlight.

Ingredients:
2/3 cup Liquid Castile Soap
1/4 cup Raw, Unfiltered Honey
2 teaspoons Oil (jojoba, almond, sesame, or olive)
1 teaspoon Vitamin E Oil
25 drops of Bergamot oil
25 drops of Coriander oil

Directions:
Pour all ingredients into a bottle and shake vigorously. To use, squirt directly onto a loofa, washcloth, or directly onto skin.

Venomous Tentacula Foot Cream

Do your feet require a flesh eating plant to bring them back to life? Use Venomous Tentacula Foot Cream scented with hyssop to put your best feet forward.

Ingredients:
1/4 cup Shea Butter
1/4 cup Coconut Oil
2 tablespoons Olive Oil
8 drops of Hyssop Oil
7 drops of Orange Oil

Directions:
Melt Shea butter and coconut oil in a pot on low heat until melted.

Add olive oil and let cool to room temperature.

Mix in hyssop oils and orange oil and beat until creamy (about 5 minutes).

Mandragora Foot Cream

Have you been petrified by the sight of your feet?
Then the right choice is Mandragora Foot Cream,
blended with lavender and chamomile, it will make
your feet feel revived.

Ingredients:
1/4 cup Shea Butter
1/4 cup Coconut Oil
2 tablespoons Olive Oil
8 drops of Lavender Oil
7 drops of Chamomile Oil

Directions:
Melt Shea butter and coconut oil in a pot on low heat until melted.

Add olive oil and let cool to room temperature.

Mix in lavender and chamomile oils and beat until creamy (about 5 minutes).

Sherbet Lemon Lip Balm

Find the favorite candy of Albus Dumbledore now in lip balm form. Make your lips tangy and sweet with Sherbet Lemon Lip Balm.

Ingredients:
2 teaspoons Coconut Oil
1 teaspoon Beeswax
3 drops of Vitamin E Oil
1/2 teaspoon Honey
2-3 drops of Lemon Oil

Directions:
Mix all ingredients together thoroughly.

Transfer to a lip balm tube or pot (feel free to reuse your old lip balm pots or tubes).

Chocolate Frog Lip Balm

Want lips that make you want to jump for joy? Then
Chocolate Frog Lip Balm is for you. Collector's cards
not included.

Ingredients:
2 teaspoons Coconut Oil
1 teaspoon Beeswax
3 drops of Vitamin E Oil
1/2 teaspoon Honey
2-3 drops of Chocolate Flavoring Oil
A pinch of Cocoa Powder for coloring

Directions:
Mix all ingredients together thoroughly.

Transfer to a lip balm tube or pot (feel free to reuse your old lip balm pots or tubes).

Fizzing Whizbees Lip Balm

Ever feel like you need to levitate? Get as close as you
can with Fizzing Whizbees Lip Balm.
Tastes just like orange sherbet.

Ingredients:
2 teaspoons Coconut Oil
1 teaspoon Beeswax
3 drops of Vitamin E Oil
1/2 teaspoon Honey
2-3 drops of Orange Oil

Directions:
Mix all ingredients together thoroughly.

Transfer to a lip balm tube or pot (feel free to reuse your old lip balm pots or tubes).

Pumpkin Pastie Lip Balm

Dreaming of the Honeydukes trolley on the Hogwarts Express? Pumpkin Pastie Lip Balm can take you there and give you those kissably smooth lips you want.

Ingredients:
2 teaspoons Coconut Oil
1 teaspoon Beeswax
3 drops of Vitamin E Oil
1/2 teaspoon Honey
2-3 drops of Pumpkin Flavoring Oil
Turmeric for color

Directions:
Mix all ingredients together thoroughly.

Transfer to a lip balm tube or pot (feel free to reuse your old lip balm pots or tubes).

Peppermint Toad Lip Balm

Want a refreshing cool for your lips? Peppermint Toad Lip Balm is the way to go. Good news it won't hop in your stomach like the real candy.

Ingredients:
2 teaspoons Coconut Oil
1 teaspoon Beeswax
3 drops of Vitamin E Oil
1/2 teaspoon Honey
2-3 drops of Peppermint Essential Oils
A pinch of Red Beet Powder for a natural red color

Directions:
Mix all ingredients together thoroughly.

Transfer to a lip balm tube or pot (feel free to reuse your old lip balm pots or tubes).

Bertie Bott's Every Flavor Lip Balm

We can't actually pack every flavor into our Bertie Bott's Every Flavor Lip Plumping Balm; so we chose the strongest flavor of cinnamon. Get large beautiful lips and confidence with just one lip balm.

Ingredients:
2 teaspoons Coconut Oil
1 teaspoon Beeswax
3 drops of Vitamin E Oil
1/2 teaspoon Honey
2-3 drops of Cinnamon Oils
A pinch of Red Beet Powder for a natural red color

Directions:
Mix all ingredients together thoroughly.

Transfer to a lip balm tube or pot (feel free to reuse your old lip balm pots or tubes).

Lav Lav Fragrance Lotion Bars

Relax into your new smooth skin with Lav Lav, a fragrance by Lavender Brown. Lavender scented, of course, you will feel refreshed and balanced after every use.

This lotion is solid at room temperature and looks like a soap bar. But when you rub it on, the warmth from your skin melts a small amount of the lotion and leaves you with a very thin, ultra-moisturizing layer.

Ingredients:
1 cup Coconut Oil
1 cup Cold-Pressed Shea Butter or Cocoa Butter
1 cup + 1 tablespoon Beeswax
1 teaspoon Vitamin E Oil
4-5 drops of Lavender oil

Directions:
Combine ingredients (except lavender oil) inside a quart-sized mason jar. Leave the lid loosely placed on the jar. Place the mason jar inside a pan with 1 inch of water in it.

Turn the heat on medium and stir the ingredients until completely melted.

Remove jar from heat and stir in lavender oil.

Carefully pour liquid into a square pan or baking molds.

Allow bars to cool. Then pop them out of their mold. If you poured them into the square pan, cut the bars out like you would brownies.

Won Won Fragrance Lotion Bar

Feel anchored and grounded with Lavender Brown's
new lotion bar for men, WonWon. Blended with
vetiver, this woodsy smelling lotion will leave you
relaxed.

This lotion is solid at room temperature and looks like
a soap bar. But when you rub it on, the warmth from
your skin melts a small amount of the lotion and
leaves you with a very thin, ultra-moisturizing layer.

Ingredients:
1 cup Coconut Oil
1 cup Cold-Pressed Shea Butter or Cocoa Butter
1 cup + 1 tablespoon Beeswax
1 teaspoon Vitamin E Oil
5-6 drops of Vetiver oil

Directions:
Combine ingredients (except vetiver oil) inside a quart-sized mason jar. Leave the lid loosely placed on the jar. Place the mason jar inside a pan with 1 inch of water in it.

Turn the heat on medium and stir the ingredients until completely melted.

Remove jar from heat and stir in veviter oil.

Carefully pour liquid into a square pan or baking molds.

Allow bars to cool. Then pop them out of their mold. If you poured them into the square pan, cut the bars out like you would brownies.

Whomping Willow Mud Mask

Has your face felt a little too oily lately?
Then use the Whomping Willow Mud Mask to get
your skin back to its natural glow.
Guaranteed to not beat you with its branches.

Ingredients:
2 tablespoons Coconut Oil
1/4 cup Bentonite Clay
8 capsules Activated Charcoal
1 tablespoon Aloe Vera Gel
4 oz. Chamomile Tea
5 drops of Tea Tree Oil

Directions:
Melt coconut oil into a liquid.

Cut the charcoal capsules in half and dump the contents into a bowl. Combine the rest of the ingredients, EXCEPT tea, into the bowl and mix.

Slowly whisk in the cooled tea until you reach a creamy consistency.

Scoop mixture into a lidded glass jar and refrigerate for 1 hour.

Store unused portion in refrigerator for up to 1 month.

Devil's Snare Mud Mask

Want to get out of that dark damp environment and
no longer have constricted skin? Use Devil's Snare
Mud Mask, and step out into the sun.

Ingredients:
2 tablespoons Coconut Oil
1/4 cup Bentonite Clay
8 capsules Activated Charcoal
1 tablespoon Aloe Vera Gel
4 oz. Chamomile Tea
5 drops of Orange Essential Oil

Directions:
Melt coconut oil into a liquid.

Cut the charcoal capsules in half and dump the contents into a bowl. Combine the rest of the ingredients, EXCEPT tea, into the bowl and mix.

Slowly whisk in the cooled tea until you reach a creamy consistency.

Scoop mixture into a lidded glass jar and refrigerate for 1 hour.

Store unused portion in refrigerator for up to 1 month.

Gryffindor Pore No More Salt Scrub

Do you want to feel brave like a proud lion and be strong of will? Gryffindor Pore No More Salt Scrub will heighten your confidence and strengthen your skin. Scented with Cedarwood and Rose, it's the right blend to make you feel uplifted and powerful.

Ingredients:
2 cups Coconut Oil
1 cup Epsom salts
5 drops of Cedarwood Essential Oil
5 drops of Rose Essential Oil

Directions:
Mix all ingredients together and store in an airtight lidded jar.

Hufflepuff Amazing Face Stuff
Salt Scrub

Are you a kind and tolerant person that just wants to relax a little? Then Hufflepuff Amazing Face Stuff is the right product for you. Scented with lemongrass and green tea, you will feel full of vitality and ready for the Quidditch pitch.

Ingredients:
2 cups Coconut Oil
1 cup Epsom Salts
5 drops of Lemongrass Essential Oil
5 drops of Green Tea

Directions:
Mix all ingredients together and store in an airtight lidded jar.

Ravenclaw Goodbye Flaw Salt Scrub

Are you super stressed from your OWLs or NEWTs?
Do you need to just relax a little and feel normal? Then
Ravenclaw Goodbye Flaw is the salt scrub for you,
scented with lavender and mint you will feel refreshed
for the summer holiday.

Ingredients:
2 cups Coconut Oil
1 cup Epsom Salts
5 drops of Lavender Essential Oil
5 drops of Mint Essential Oil

Directions:
Mix all ingredients together and store in an airtight lidded jar.

Slytherin to Smoother Skin Salt Scrub

Do you need a salt scrub for your cunning personality? Then Slytherin to Smoother Skin is your best choice. Scented with lime and clary sage, your skin will be exfoliated and you will feel centered and determined once again.

Ingredients:
2 cups Coconut Oil
1 cup Epsom Salts
5 drops of Lime Essential Oil
5 drops of Clary Sage Essential Oil

Directions:
Mix all ingredients together and store in an airtight lidded jar.

Gilderoy Lockhart's
Oatmeal Lavender Bath Soak

Want to relax and look fabulous? Cannot guarantee fame and fortune, but Gilderoy Lockhart's Oatmeal Lavender Bath Soak is definitely the right direction. (Makes enough for about 5 baths)

Ingredients:
4 cups Plain Old Fashioned Oats
3 tablespoons Dried Lavender (look for "food grade" or "culinary")
1 cup Baking Soda

Directions:
Grind all ingredients in a food processer or blender until very fine and powdery.

Distribute into 5 bags or jars.

To use: Pour into running water and soak for 15-30 minutes.

Gillyweed Face Mask

Seaweed will leave your skin smooth and youthful.
With Gillyweed Face Mask, you'll feel so transformed
you'll think you can breath under water.

Ingredients:
3-4 sheets of Dried Seaweed
1-2 tablespoons Water
1 teaspoon Honey

Directions:
Grind seaweed in a food processor, coffee bean grinder, or blender until it's fine and powdery.

Mix the seaweed, water, and honey until you get a thick, creamy consistency.

To use: Apply mask to your face and leave in place for 20 minutes. Rinse with lukewarm water.

Flaming Kiwi Facial Scrub

Want to knock out those harmful effects of the sun and slow down the appearance of wrinkles? The Flaming Kiwi Facial Scrub will leave your skin looking youthful, and make you feel like you've just spent all your money in Honeydukes.

77

Ingredients:
3 Ripe Kiwis
4 tablespoons Greek Yogurt
1 tablespoon Olive Oil
2 tablespoons Orange Juice

Directions:
Mix all ingredients in a blender or food processor.

Use immediately or store in the fridge for up to 3 days.

Madam Pudifoot's
Rose Water Skin Toner

Have a romantic trip to the tea shop with Madam
Pudifoot's Rose Water Skin Toner, and it will leave
your face smelling wonderful and
feeling blissfully clean.

Ingredients:
1 cup Rose Petals
2 cups Water

Directions:
Pour water in saucepan and add the rose petals. Boil for 15 minutes.

Strain rose water into a jar. It's ready to use!

Keep in the fridge for up to 2 weeks.

Butterbeer Body Butter

Travel back to the Three Broomsticks with
Butterbeer Body Butter.

Your skin will be left silky smooth and relaxed.

Ingredients:
1/2 cup Cold-Pressed Shea Butter
1/2 cup Cocoa Butter
1/2 cup Coconut Oil
1/2 cup Jojoba Oil
10 drops of Vanilla
20 Butterscotch Fragrance Oil

Directions:
Combine ingredients (except butterscotch oil) inside a quart-sized mason jar. Leave the lid loosely placed on the jar. Place the mason jar inside a pan with 1 inch of water in it.

Turn the heat on medium and stir the ingredients until completely melted.

Remove jar from heat and stir in butterscotch oil.

Put jar in fridge and let ingredients cool for 1 hour. The mixture should be beginning to harden, but is still soft.

Using a hand mixer, whip it up for 10 minutes, until fluffy.

Put it back in the fridge for 15 minutes to set.

Now it's ready to put in a pretty glass jar!

Note: If the temperature is above 75, the body butter will melt, so if your house is kept that warm, keep yours in the fridge.

We hope you enjoyed the magic of potion-making in your own kitchen. We also hope you didn't burn anything, like fingers or cats.

If you have any questions or comments, email us at info@razzberrybooks.com

Happy wizarding!